dead of night

chris mc geown

Cover art by Natasha Genge

Inspired by the artworks of
Jen Klinedist

ISBN: 1543012604
ISBN-13: 978-1543012606

CONTENTS

Acknowledgments	i-v
1 A.M.	page 1-44
2 A.M.	page 45-84
3 A.M.	page 85-130
4 A.M.	page 131-171
5 A.M.	page 172-205

DEDICATION

To my mom who never left
To my dad who never gave up
To my brother for keeping me happy
To my sisters for keeping me sane.

1 A.M.

I crave stillness,
And yet I fear the moment
Stillness turns into boredom,
And the moment boredom
Turns into loneliness.

home

The words complicate things,
But all I know
Is that she smells like heaven
And she feels like home.

closed off

Some people
Walk around
So closed off
Because
There are things
Inside of them
That could swallow them
Whole.

romance

People talk of love
And comfort
As though they are
Mutually exclusive;
As though two souls
Sitting as two,
Thinking as one,
Is not the most
Beautifully romantic experience
There is.

clay

Humans are not glass,
That gets broken
Into millions of pieces,
Each one smaller than the last;
An impossible jigsaw puzzle
That gets broken beyond repair.

We are clay,
Molded by the decisions
Of our own hands—
We may decide to start over
Or be smushed into the ground,
But we have everything in us
To rise up again
And create something beautiful.

skin deep

I wish my tears
Would erode
My skin
And expose
What lies
Beneath.

new years eve

What is new years eve
But a time to reflect;
Spend it with people you love,
Spend it with people you know,
Spend it alone,
Spend it in love,
Spend it happy,
Spend it sad,
I've done each one—
And it doesn't really matter,
The only thing that matters
Is how much can change in a year,
And so you can too.

the simple truth about obstacles (as told by the seas)

The seas know
That even the smallest stream
Can break through the biggest barrier,
All it takes is constant motion
And time.

the builder

No wonder you feel so
Down
With walls built so
High.

star-gazing

Mental illnesses
Are constellations
Of the mind—
Most people won't
See them
Unless you point
Them out.

a letter to the loves I have lost

To everyone I have ever loved
And lost,
I'm sorry.

history lessons

Sometimes I don't get
Forgive and forget,
For those that don't know history
Are doomed to repeat it.

plain sight

The best way
To hide
In plain sight
Is to hide
Behind
Words.

relationships

Know the difference
Between those who stay
To feed the soil
And those who come
To grab the fruit.

nostalgia

Nostalgia can be a dangerous thing;
Trapping people in moments
And memories,
All the while
Time moving forward–
Their bodies present
Their souls stuck.

amateur cartography

My hands have
Mapped out
Every inch
Of your body,
Yet still
I find myself
Lost.

dead of night

I gauge
My emotional state
By seeing whether
I find comfort
Or sadness
In the still calm
Of night.

sorry

I say sorry
For simple,
Seemingly innocuous
Things,
Not because I am too polite,
But because at one time
Someone made me
Feel like I should be.

temporary

Love highlights our search
For permanent beauty
In a world
Where everything
Is temporary.

baby blue

Secrets swept
Under rugs;
Tears trickled down
From one generation
To another,
Creating fears,
Coloring their minds
Blue.

post-mortem

Show me
The skeletons
Of two men
And tell me
Which man
Was greater?

beautiful

To be able
To find beauty
You must know beauty;
To know beauty,
You must have beauty
Within.

please hold on

Please hold on
I almost lost you
Now I worry;
I worry there will not be
Enough time
To make up for all the things
I've done wrong,
Enough time
To give you everything
That you deserve;
Please hold on,
I almost lost you
But I gained a new view
On mortality
That has changed my reality—
Time is precious
And so are you,
Please hold on.

mystery

You shed light
On my disappearance
Into the night;
There is hope in mystery
Now it's just sad.

gone

Her body confessed to things
That her mouth dare not speak,
And yet still I waited for the words;
I knew that she was gone
Long before she left.

present

When you stop judging,
You stop focusing
On what could be,
And start seeing the beauty
In what is.

lost

I tried to convince myself
That I wasn't running away,
Until I looked back
And was lost.

supernova

I was waiting
For the stars
To align,
Without realizing
The light
From those stars
Were projections
From suns
Who died
Long ago.

the hard exterior

People see the hard shells of others
And don't understand
That it's not there by choice;
For the hardest thing is
That at one time
That shell was necessary.

la bella luna

The moon knows
That it need not shine
As bright as the sun
To be beautiful.

haunted

I can't sleep,
Haunted
By the lives
I'm choosing
Not
To lead.

baggage

I ask her
If she still loves me
Because I've never seen
A love
That lasts.

the simple truth about pipelines (as told by the trees)

The trees know

That before oil and paper

That water was the currency

Of life—and without

Water

Neither

Oil

Nor

Paper

Will

Matter.

goodbye

I had a vision
Of how our last meeting would go,
We would hug
And I would know
That you lived a good life
And were ready to go,
And you would know
That you were loved,
Especially by me;
But as I sit across from you
With you scared to leave,
And me scared for you to go,
I wish not to stop time,
But to rewind it;
To anticipate your troubles
And cure them
Before they would start—
But unfortunately
That is impossible
Because life is imperfect like that,
Just like goodbyes.

uncivil wars

Why is it
That we can all imagine
Worlds
Greater
Than the one
We've created?

your ideal lover

I see the way you look at me,
You see worlds inside of me,
You see a beautiful life,
But you don't see the cracks,
Or the ruins from collapse;
You see me as you want to see me,
But not as I am.

you've changed

You left a hole in my heart
That even your return
Could not fill;
You've changed,
But more importantly,
So have I.

twice shy

All that remained
Was the scar,
And the fear
It could happen again.

hang on

If you still love someone
After they have left you
Know that you are capable
Of great love,
And deserve the same
In return.

empty

Sometimes I miss
The parts
I saw of you
When you were
Empty too.

2 A.M.

My heart tender
I surrender to the night;
Take me wherever you want,
Just leave me anywhere
But here.

to the disillusioned and the brokenhearted

What you saw
In them
Was nothing
But a reflection
Of your own beautiful love,
Stay strong.

sweet nothings

Kind words,
And soft curves
Drew him in;
Like a moth to a flame,
That's surprised
When it's burned.

dance, dance, dance

I move perfectly
Through all
The motions
And yet
I feel nothing—
Is this dancing
Or dying?

freedom

Oppress the truths of others
And none of us shall be free.

futility

There's some sort
Of beauty
In the madness of
Futility;
The voluntary ignorance—
The hope
That accompanies
A doomed desperation.

unique

The problem is
We want
The same things
As everyone else,
But we want
To experiences things
Like no one
Else has.

old photos

Old photos make me uncomfortable;
The exposure of time,
Exposing the past joy
Hidden beneath future pain.

A reminder that you can't rewind,
And that sometimes time is unkind,
And that photos fade fast,
And that things never last.

easy

Loving you
Wasn't easy,
But most good things
Never are.

masterpiece

The clothes and jewelry
Aren't the artwork,
That's what lies beneath;
Your body's not the canvas,
It’s the whole goddamn
Masterpiece.

invisible scars

When my father left,
I turned the light in my room
On,
Then off;
On,
And then off—
I didn't trust
When it went off,
That it would come back on.

wounds

Wounds opened
By words
Are the toughest
To close.

wings

Wings can be seen
As a blessing
Or a curse
Depending on
The height of the tree
And the disposition
Of the bird.

the simple truth about beauty (as told by the trees)

Often it is the trees

Who are a little crooked—

A little weird— who last the longest.

They don't fit any conventional need

So they continue to grow

Until they

Are

The

Tallest,

Weirdest,

Most

Beautiful

Trees

In

The woods.

okay

I thought you'd be able
To see it on my face,
To hear it in my voice,
To understand the
Words unspoken,
Yet confessed
By the original language,
To spare me the courage
I lost from these days
To speak up and say
That I am not okay.

the giver

I put my heart
Into the hands of another,
Without realizing,
The heart is to be shared,
Not given.

sounds of silence

Sometimes the silence sounds
Like echoes
Of every word I never said
But should have,
And even the slightest sound
Is relief.

be assured

It is the plants
That take the most shit
Which bear the richest fruits.

a break in the clouds

The clouds receded
Just enough
To bathe in the sun
And convince myself
That I am okay.

classified

So many people
Let the labels
They are given
Become them;
Don't let one person's
Simplicity
Define the complex
Beauty
That exists within you.

what is normal?

When you find yourself starting to break,
The vulnerability
Can seep out through the cracks
At the most inopportune times;
Asking for help in all the wrong places,
Shouting into the void;
Seeking help within normal society
Where the social norm isn't normal,
Where we can't express our emotions
But instead must be 'okay'.

truth be told

I never really wanted
To die—
I just wanted someone to see
How much of a struggle
It was
For me to live.

balancing act

I am sturdy in body,
Unbalanced in mind;
I stand so tall,
But I fall so easy.

wither

You wished to take
The flowers from my garden
To make them yours,
Only to watch them wither
And die.

deafening

I fill the silences
With thoughts of you,
For that is where you live now;
You were the first to say goodbye,
As someone always is.

textbook

The ivory towers,
The land-locked blues,
The oceans of hues,
The tattooed bruise.

stuck

The beating of my heart,
The tick-tick of my old brown clock,
The pitter-patter of the rain on my window;
Everything around me is in constant motion,
While I sit here,
Stuck.

flower bed

Where the world
Breaks us
Will be
Where
The flowers
Will grow.

piece by piece

Break me down
To my pieces
And I am nothing
But bad luck
And good intentions.

escape artist

Sometimes
You don't realize
How much
You need an escape
Until you find one.

the handy man's hands

It is the mind
Of the man
With the scars
On his hands
Who will carefully
Craft
The most beautiful
Things.

starving

Attention
Can look a lot
Like love
And affection
For the soul
That's starved
Of both.

tipsy

I drink you in
So my soul
Might dance
Again.

heartbreak

No matter
How hard
The loving
Gets,
The leaving
Is never
Easy.

tension

I have an exhaustion
That evades sleep and rest,
Which begs solitude
And reflection;
The knots have built-up,
And there's a tension inside of me
That I need to work out
Alone.

lost

Love
Is never
Learned
Until it is
Lost.

faraway

My past life
And lover
Have both left me
Lost.

true

Let the skies open
And the tears
Fall—
I feel
Trivial enough
To be true.

present tense

Sometimes
I feel trapped
In the present
By a future
I can't imagine
And a past
I can't escape.

closure

There is no closure
In watching things slip away
Slowly
Like an unnamed boat
Carrying namesaked lovers
To unknown lands
Before time of
Telephones
And text,
Grasping
At an image
Of a ship in the distance—
But memories fresh,
Wondering if their loves
Will come back
Or if their ship
Will come.

3 A.M.

Sometimes I feel
So ashamed of the past
And afraid of the future,
And I wonder who I am.

acceptance

No red flags
Or white flags
Just people,
And problems,
And love.

leaving

How many of us,
Through no fault
Of our own,
Have learned
Leaving
Before we learned
Loving?

escape

I went around the world,
But the only place
I could escape myself
Was with you.

ebb and flow

Your presence like a wave,
Washing in over me,
Finding the cracks
In my hard surface;
Filling me up
Then leaving–
Slowly
Breaking me
Down.

rain song

She flirted
With the rain
But fear being
Swallowed up
By the sea.

angel

Somewhere
Between heaven
And hell
I found you,
Bearer of beauty
And bad news;
An angel.

sensitive

To be sensitive
Is a strength
Many mistake
For weakness;
To see the vulnerability
In life
And not want to exploit it
But nurture it
Is a gift;
For one must see the cracks
In order to fix
The soul.

insignificance

At night,
When the sky fades to black
And opens up to millions of stars
And galaxies I will never know,
They humble my problems
And humble my mind;
The liberating feeling of freedom
That comes with insignificance.

the simple truth about growth (as told by the trees)

Sometimes a

Tree must lose its

Dead and dying

Limbs

In

Order

To

Grow.

the gardener

You are not a flower;
You are so much more
Than your roots
And your beauty,
And your ability to create life—
There are gardens
That lie within you
That most men
Could not begin
To imagine.

easy

So easily
The soul hides
While bodies
And bravado
Intertwine.

patience

Wait long enough
And most mountains
Move themselves.

firefly

Find me again
Beneath the moonlight—
If life is darkness
Our love is light

flawless

Her humble
Beauty hiding
Behind her
Flawless facade.

Fools who foolishly
Tried to climb
Over walls well built,
And found themselves falling.

Men left lamenting
If it was her
Or the facade
They couldn't get over.

on the mend

Healing
May not be
Pretty,
Or painless,
Or quick;
But it is
Inevitable.

past and pending

Look to someone's past,
Not to define them,
But to understand them.

intoxicated

The drinks
Were my excuse
To be intoxicatingly
Impractical
About life
And love.

facade

If one day
My walls do fall
Will I be naked,
Or free?

dead of night

Sometimes
In the dead of night
I feel utterly and completely
Alone;
I can't tell
If it's because I'm broken
Or human.

distance

Sometimes pushing
People away
Is your heads way
Of doing
What the heart
Can't bring itself to do.

starry night

The stars keep me company
In the dead of night,
For they are dead too;
Ghosts of galaxies,
Cemeteries of civilizations
Never known;
And so I whisper my secrets to them,
Knowing they are gone,
And by the time my words reach them,
I will be too.

the cleansing truth about deep breathes (as told by the trees)

The trees know

About the importance of

Inhaling all of the toxic things

It is given, and exhaling life;

Slowly

Letting

It

Go

Out

Into

The

Universe.

wisdom

For some reason
People seem to mix up
Getting locked into the serious
Expectations of societies dogmatic
Conventions
With growing up.
Be immature, find humor,
Be light-hearted and gentle;
Approach things with
The childlike expectation
That they will be fun;
You may never 'grow up'—
But you will grow wise.

gaslight anthem

How cruel it is
To deny yourself something
Which is born from you,
Something so personal
And pure
As a feeling.

worthy

You lost your way
Not your worth.

drink of choice

She was my drink of choice,
And I was never satisfied
Until I no longer knew who I was
Or how I got there.

wildfire

Your love burned too bright
For a gasoline heart
On a warm summer's night.

many a moon

When did I go
From being so bright eyed
Listening intently
In the classroom,
Hopeful—
To staring with dead eyes
Taking orders
At a job,
Jaded—
The nights
Used to make everything seem
So separate,
Yet here I stand,
Some sort of exhausted
Accumulation of the days.

fools gold

What is more foolish
Than those who value objects
More than life itself;
Perhaps even real gold
Is fools gold
In the end.

that art of remembering

Patchwork pieces
Of a patterned past,
Torn little by little
And filled in with blue.

paradise lost

I wish to see you again
Underneath the moonlight
And I will fill the silences
With all the things I never said,
But should have–
And it will feel like home again
If only for a second,
Before you disappear,
And home is lost again.

healing

Band-aids and alcohol
Might help,
But at the end of the day
Only you
Can heal yourself.

dead silence

I used to speak my words
To the winds at night,
But recently I've stopped—
I realize that I have been saying
Nothing,
And I had been saying
Nothing
For some time;
For what does the man who is lost
Have to say?
Perhaps my silence
Speaks
More than my empty words
Ever could.

the naked truth

Let the emotions rise inside of you,
And set them free,
For the feelings that are kept and caged
Do far more damage
Than any truth
Ever could.

memories

Strangely
You may
Love a memory
More
Than you loved
A moment.

life

You painted beauty
On my canvas—
I called it art,
You called it life.

deathbed

I have never met
A person
On their deathbed
Who says
They wished
They worried more
And loved less.

cast away

It was only once you left for good
That I realized
I've always sort of missed you—
That you were never fully there
To begin with.

moon-child

You light up
My nights
In a way
That no sun
Ever could.

true love

True love
Doesn't hold
A hurt
It can't heal.

sadness

You can't always see
The pure humanity
In happiness,
But you can always see it
In sadness–
And that's what makes sadness
So beautiful–
It might not be pretty
But at least it's true.

the simple truth about growth (as told by the trees)

The trees know

That growth happens

Even on the the

Darkest of nights

In

The

Coldest

Of

Winters.

the entertainer

I had been
Putting on
The same damn show,
Night after night,
And no one caught on.

worlds inside

Relying on
One person
To fill you up
Assumes
That you
Aren't already
Full;
There are
Whole worlds
Inside of you,
One person
Won't
Change that.

the broken

Those who have
Been broken
Are the best,
Because they know
What you need
To be put back
Together.

drop in the glass

He drinks
To forget
Scarred memories past;
The problems at hand
Just a drop
In the glass.

monsters

Monsters are those
Who let the bitterness of the world
Become them.

the democratic process

We closed our eyes
To the cool comfort of democracy,
Awakened
With eyes too tired
For corrupt commoditization–
Domains dominated by dictators
Who protect and push
'Democracy'.

defenses

The drama of her
Draws you in,
The conflict
Between sad eyes
And a beautiful smile—
A story,
A mystery,
A wall worth climbing.

morning routine

Every morning
Begins
With a glass of water,
A pill,
And a humbling reminder
That sometimes
Everyone needs
A little help.

diamonds

You must relieve
Some of this pressure
You put on yourself,
We are not the earth
And this pressure will not
Turn us into diamonds;
Under such a weight
All humans are destined
To crumble.

build me up, buttercup

I have been
Built up
And torn down
By so many people
I realized
The truest way
To build anything
Within myself
Was by myself.

day in, day out

I need time alone—
For the mask I wear
Is heavy,
And when worn
For too long
It always starts
To bring me down.

rings

Expensive rings
On wrinkled fingers
Remind me
No amount
Of material goods
Can slow
The inevitability of time.

far-sighted

You said everything
Looks better
From a distance;
For you have a beautiful mind
And think beautiful things,
And the projections
You imagine
Are far better
Than the realities
You see.

home

When I got there
I lay down
A piece of my heart;
It grew roots
And became my home
(I miss it).

depth

There is no
Such
Thing
As depth
Without
Darkness.

the simple truth about time (as told by the trees)

You can invest

In the land and the seeds

And the tools for the trees, but

Unless you invest your

Time,

Nothing

Of

Consequence

Shall

Grow.

outliers

There are always outliers
In statistical sets,
That refuse to accept
The destiny
That society
Has laid out for them.

scabs

Some people can't
Help but pick at
Old wounds
Until the dry crustiness
Of the scab
Becomes them.

the love/hate relationship

If people were as good
At receiving and recognizing love and affection
As they were disdain and hatred,
The world would be a much happier place;
There is so much love
That
Just
Falls
Through
The
Cracks.

sleepless in Toronto

It was your voice
The lullaby
To my sleepless nights—
Keeping me barely alive,
In the dead of night.

perpetually progressing

To try and definitively find yourself
Is like trying to catch your own shadow—
As soon as you've lunged at it,
It is in a different place entirely;
So I seek not to find myself,
Rather to try and listen to myself,
And accept myself as I am.

old records

When I grow old
I wish to be like a record;
Every line on my body will tell a story,
And they may not all be happy,
But when you run your hands over mine
We won't have to speak,
But they will make you feel comfortable
In knowing I made it,
And so you will too.

vested interests

The cruel twist
Is that the more time,
Effort,
And energy
You give to someone,
The more you care about them,
Irregardless of the time,
Effort,
And energy
They give back to you.

pining

Sometimes
I catch a glimpse
Of the person
I used to be;
The bittersweet feeling
Of remembering
Everything
I'd yet to lose.

the simple truth about being (as told by the trees)

The trees know
That beauty isn't found in
Standing the tallest, Or in
Having the most leaves,
Or in having people stop
And stare;
The
Trees
Know
That
Beauty
Is
Simply
Found
In
Being.

peace of mind

There is no eternal high,
Or eternal low;
All that I ask
Is that I find peace
In the silences
Through it all.

the art of letting go

Perhaps some things are only beautiful
Because they are temporary.

evolution

One day
I hope another species
Evolves to speak and think
Like humans,
Learns our language,
And tells us
To fuck off.

wings

Too often we focus
On the beauty
In the wings
Of the butterfly
Without waiting
To see
How well
It flies.

linguistics

Love speaks to
The soul
In a language
The brain
Can't comprehend.

the simple truth about light (as told by the trees)

The trees know
That no matter how
Uneven the ground it grows on
May seem, that it must always
Stretch towards the light;
It trusts that the
Sun
Will
Nurture
It,
And
It
Trusts
That
It's
Roots
Will
Hold it.

the ghosts that lie within the skin

The wounds
will hurt you,

But the scars
Can haunt you.

possession

Too many men
Trying to take
Ownership
Over the masterpieces
They've found.

saviour

It is okay
To leave
The people
You cannot save,
But please do not hurt
Them on your way out—
It is not your fault
You cannot save them,
But it is not their fault
Either.

metamorphosis

I have become
The bug
Of Kafka—
Bound in convention,
Drowned by passion—
Some life.

moonstruck

Grapes raised to raisin,
Soul stuck in a mind
So brazen;
Tough to know,
Harder to love,
But callous souls glow
Under shooting stars above.

skin

What is more
Maligned
And meaningless
Than skin?

in a dream

I imagined
That I was beautiful
And you were
Free.

depth

Mostly our lives
Are too short
To know
The depth
Of our meaning;
And yet
Too long
Not to know
The depth
Of our pain.

time-bomb

I remember
When our goodbyes
Were temporary,
And our reunions were joyful.

moonshine

It was moonshine
Dressed as
Wine
And by the end
Of the night
I could've sworn
I saw how utterly magical
Our star looked
From out in the universe,
And it was
So beautiful,
I cried.

5 a.m.

I lingered on
As we sat
In silence—
There was
Nothing
Left to say
But goodbye.

left

I knew I would get lost in you

So I left.

inside out

The words rose
And fell
Inside of me—
Waves crashing
In the midst of your storm,
Just begging for release;
But you left too soon,
And now those words lie dormant,
Slowly rotting me
From the inside out.

stay

For all your faults
You never left,
And that's more
Than I can say
For most.

milk and honey

How much blood, sweat and tears
Must we give to a government
Who squandered our land,
Flowing with milk and honey,
To build up mansions
On our backs,
Beaten and broken;
Fortunes made on too much blood,
Too much sweat,
And too many tears—
How can they still enjoy
That milk and honey.

reckless

Empowerment
Without education
Is a dangerous
And destructive
Proposition.

hangover

It was your wine
Which always tasted
The sweetest,
That left me
The sickest.

black coffee

I was talking to my dad,
About two women
When he looked at my coffee
An iced latte,
Equivalent to two creams
And two sugars
Light and sweet;
He always
Drank his coffee strong
And black,
He said he needed
The darkness of the coffee
To justify the sweetness
Of the sugar—
He said mine was fine
At first
But reckoned by the end of it,
I'd be hating myself,
And that no one could take
That kind of sweetness, without darkness
'Your speaking in metaphor,
Your point is too obvious'
I murmured,
'I know it's obvious,
But you want it to be meaningful'
And that was all he said.

where the heart is

I don't want to miss you anymore
But I don't want to forget you,
My heart still aches—
I just wish you'd come home.

all of me

If you love me
Love
All of me,
Especially the parts
That need it most.

rush

Kiss me like the waves
Kiss the shore—
Briefly and beautifully,
With reckless abandon.

boundless

I am water;
With pressure
I take any form
Convention demands of me,
But ultimately
I am most at ease
In the vastness I have
When I take no form at all.

shooting star

You were

Shooting

For the

Stars

But got

Lost

In the

High.

symphony

My mind is quiet at times,
Loud and overwhelming at others,
It is a symphony which knows
It needs both
To be beautiful.

selfless

Some love
Will be given
And not reciprocated
This is the hardest
Most important love
To give.

home

There's so many people
Wishing
For paradise
Without realizing
They're home.

not enough

How many times
Must we be broken down
Than told
We're not enough?

sing me to sleep

Sometimes I stay up
And wait for the birds
To sing me to sleep.

how to fall in love again

1. let go
2. live

free

You must only be strong
If you carry those things around with you;
Let them out
And let them go—
Be weak
If it means you'll be free.

false dichotomies

I'm not happy
Or sad.

I'm not good
Or bad.

I'm not introverted
Or extroverted.

I'm not masculine
Or feminine.

I am not straight
Or gay.

I am not sane
Or insane.

I am a just a person,
Trying to define myself
In black and white terms
In a dark grey world.

raindrop

You are rain to the water
Dancing briefly—
Beautifully—
Before you disappear.

oh, fortune

Fortune frowns
On the man who
Is not bound
But still
Stuck.

mindfulness

Abandon the flower
And it dies,
Abandon the weed
And it grows.

dawn

I was born
To two people
Falling apart
From each other
And themselves,
And as I fall apart
Inside
I can't help
But see it as anything
Other than inevitable.

you were wrong

You said
There were parts
Of me
That no one
Could love—
And I believed you
For a long time—
Until I learned
To love
Myself.

the sea

Some nights
I wished
To become the sea,
And imagined
All of the beautiful
Places I would go,
And all of the beautiful
Things I would become a part of—
Essential, beautiful,
Interesting—
Always moving
But never lost.

frozen

Fill me up,
Then turn to ice
And watch me
Crack
Apart.

craving

Sadly,
Great amounts
Of pain are inevitable
For those of us
Who crave
Great amounts
Of love.

you

Everything I want
And fear
Collide
In you.

meander

The truth wells
Behind my eyes
And dances
On my lips,
But I never
Rock the boat
In hopes it never
Tips.

promise of dawn

When the sun's
At its highest
It's easy to forget
The promise of dawn,
The beauty
Of the sunrise,
And the coldness
Of the night.

the end

The only thing
That's promised
Is the end.

Thank you for reading.

Made in the USA
San Bernardino, CA
10 March 2018